Presented to

_____

On the occasion of

_____

From

_____

Date

_____

I'LL ASK MY
Grandmother
SHE'S VERY WISE

Kristen Johnson Ingram

Illustrated by Lisa Totman

PROMISE
PRESS
An Imprint of Barbour Publishing

Published by Promise Press, an imprint of Barbour Publishing, P.O. Box 719, Uhrichsville, OH 44683 http://www.barbourbooks.com

Member of the
Evangelical Christian
Publishers Association

Printed in China.

Dedication

In memory of my wonderful grandmothers,
Elizabeth Stephens Metcalfe and Jessie McJunkin Johnson

Say to wisdom,
"You are my sister,"
and call insight
your intimate friend. . .

Proverbs 7:4 *(NRSV)*

Foreword

I overheard one of my grandsons reading Edward Lear's "The Owl and the Pussycat" to his younger brother. After they were finished, little Adam asked, "But what's a runcible spoon?"

"I don't know," Andrew said. "I'll ask Grandmother. She's very wise."

Grandmothers *are* wise. They've had some time to learn how life should be lived and how children should be nurtured. They usually have at least one crackerjack skill: They can make a batch of fudge or peanut brittle in record time, or they know how to make a stubborn computer behave, or they can coax a baby to stop crying when its parents have given up.

Today's grandmothers (and substitute grandmothers) are rarely domestic or formal or sitting in rocking chairs: They're certified public accountants or telephone installers or restaurant workers; they're flaggers at street repairs, or doctors, or newspaper reporters. But they still have a mysterious and dynamic quality that makes children know a grandmother when they see one.

Wisdom:

A FOUNDATION BUILT ON THE PAST

And Adam called his wife's name Eve;
because she was the mother of all living.

Genesis 3:20

Eve is our grandmother;
we just don't have enough
"great-greats" to put
in front of her name.
Although she was unwise in the Garden,
she was wise enough to
mother the whole human race.

Every woman becomes a grandmother, whether she has biological descendants or not. She is a community elder, a repository of information and learning; she remembers what others may never know. She can be available to mothers and children of her community, to teach strategies for interaction and communication, to offer cures for warts and nosebleeds, to model power for every woman and compassion to every child. She knows she must be the example of grace and humor to her family, so she's in the church pew on Sunday morning and setting the big table on Sunday afternoon. She reads, so that her children and grandchildren read, too, hoping to find her secret of life in a book. When two children fight, a grandmother knows how to negotiate a peace and make each child feel like the winner. She teaches joy along with the trick for cooking perfect rice; she shows others how to be happy in the midst of adversity or to sew pennies in drapery hems to hold them down.

Everyone knows the healing power of a grandmother's kiss on a hurt finger. She can also heal the anger between a father and son; she can make a baby bird live to fly again, and she knows how to pray for the sick. She is girl, woman, and ancient one all at once. She's very wise.

And on that cheek, and o'er that brow,
So soft, so calm, so eloquent,
The smiles that win, the tints that glow
but tell of days in goodness spent,
A mind at peace with all below,
A heart whose love is innocent.

GEORGE GORDON, LORD BYRON
"She Walks in Beauty, Like the Night"

Other things may change us, but we start and end with family.

ANTHONY BRANDT

*C*ountless stories can be told of gratifying relationships between the generations, where love and mutual enjoyment flow from the older to the younger as from the younger to the older. The generations mix and mingle, each one living independently but drawing strength and support from the other.

Affirmative Aging: A Resource for Ministry

"Muddy," my maternal grandmother, guided her three granddaughters in the church in such a way that we are lifetime members and look back at her with reverence.

BARBARA SIMS, retired teacher

*I*t is the way I saw her on Saturday afternoons in the winter that I remember my grandmother Buechner best. She sits in her overstuffed chair with the lamp behind her unlit, though New York City is turning gray through the window. On the sill at her elbow, her squat little Philco is playing Wagner. She knows the libretto by heart as she also knows by heart how to crochet in the dusk with her silk and scissors lying on the great shelf of her bosom.

FREDERICK BUECHNER, *The Sacred Journey*

What's happened to us is that our chain of caretaking got interrupted. [During] my mom's generation. . .federal law put [the Cherokee kids] in boarding school. Cut off their hair, taught them English. . .made them spend their entire childhood in a dormitory. They got to see their people maybe twice a year. Family has always been our highest value, but that generation of kids never learned how to be in a family. The past got broken off.

BARBARA KINGSOLVER, *Pigs in Heaven*

Knowledge comes,
but wisdom lingers.

ALFRED, LORD TENNYSON, "Locksley Hall"

Bubby (Yiddish for "Grandma") was an avid bingo player, joke teller, tchotchke collector, and social dancer. She was endowed with a cackling laugh and an impressive scowl. The Brooklyn flat she shared with Grandpa Max boasted a Magnus Chord Organ and sputtering window fan, both sheathed in translucent yellowed plastic to protect against their parakeet, Poopsie. Bubby pioneered the use of the three-word contraction "tsa," as in "tsa shame" and "tsa terrible thing," during the Great Depression. She hailed from Stanislau, Austria, one of eight siblings, six of whom perished in the Nazi Holocaust.

SEAN ALTMAN, New York singer/songwriter

So Boaz took Ruth
and she became his wife.
When they came together,
the LORD made her conceive,
and she bore a son.
Then Naomi took the child
and laid him in her bosom,
and became his nurse.
The women of the neighborhood
gave him a name, saying,
"A son has been born to Naomi."
They named him Obed;
he became the father of Jesse,
the father of David.

Ruth 4:13, 16–17 (NRSV)

*N*aomi may be the most famous grandmother
in all Scripture! She was wise enough to guide
Ruth toward Boaz and his fields.
Although Obed wasn't her son's actual child,
laws in Israel declared
that this was her legal grandchild.

*Naomi's great-grandson was David,
the greatest king of Israel, and the ancestor of Jesus.*

*A family is
a place where principles are
hammered and honed
on the anvil of everyday living.*

CHARLES SWINDOLL

Grandmother

Grandmother is very old, her face is wrinkled, and her hair is quite white; but her eyes are like two stars, and they have a mild, gentle expression in them when they look at you, which does you good. She wears a dress of heavy, rich silk, with large flowers worked on it; and it rustles when she moves. And she can tell the most wonderful stories. Grandmother knows a great deal, for she was alive before father and mother—that's quite certain. She has a hymnbook with large silver clasps, which she often reads; and in the book, between the leaves, lies a rose, quite flat and dry; it is not so pretty as the roses which are standing in the glass, and yet she smiles at it most pleasantly, and tears even come into her eyes. "I wonder why Grandmother looks at the withered flower in the old book that way? Do you know?" Why, when Grandmother's tears fall upon the rose, and she is looking at it, the rose revives, and fills the room with its fragrance; the walls vanish as in a mist, and all around her is the glorious green wood, where in summer the sunlight streams through thick foliage; and Grandmother, why she is young again, a charming maiden, fresh as a rose, with round, rosy cheeks, fair, bright ringlets, and a figure pretty and graceful; but the eyes, those mild, saintly eyes, are the same—they have been left to Grandmother. At her side sits a young man, tall and strong; he gives her a rose and she smiles. Grandmother cannot smile like that now. Yes, she is smiling at the memory of that day, and many thoughts and recollections of the past; but the handsome young man is gone, and the rose has withered in the old book, and Grandmother is sitting there, again an old woman, looking down upon the withered rose in the book.

HANS CHRISTIAN ANDERSEN, 1845

*F*or you, O Lord, are my hope, my trust,
O Lord, from my youth.
Upon you I have leaned from my birth;
it was you who took me from my mother's womb.
My praise is continually of you.
I have been like a portent to many,
but you are my strong refuge.
My mouth is filled with your praise,
and with your glory all day long.
Do not cast me off in the time of old age;
do not forsake me when my strength is spent.

Psalm 71:5–9 (NRSV)

Practical Wisdom from the Past

. . .Incline thine ear unto wisdom,
and apply thine heart
to understanding.

Proverbs 2:2

My wise grandmother was full of sayings that have guided me through my entire life. They include practical things: Never leave a sinkful of dirty dishes; it makes the job twice as hard. Straighten the living room before going to bed—that way you have a head start on the day and you feel good all over. Make your bed before you leave the bedroom. Learn to cook one thing well; God never made a man who didn't like to eat. Sew on a button the minute it pops off; if you don't, you'll lose it. Always keep a well-filled larder so you can feed unexpected guests at all times. Save for a rainy day. God gets at least ten percent and the "kitty" gets five. Waste not, want not; conservation helps save our natural resources. Never throw anything useable away. It's better to have it and not need it than to need it and not have it; this applies to coats, scarves, umbrellas, and your own snacks at ball games.

Then there's manners: Write a thank-you note on the same day you receive a gift. Leave a place better than when you came. Never take your shoes off in public. Always carry a clean handkerchief. (I asked about tissues, but she said, "No, a handkerchief looks feminine.") Don't hold your clothes together with safety pins; you never know when you might be in an accident.

Now the important stuff, the inner strengths, the inner person: Anything worth doing at all is worth doing well. When you marry, be the best wife you can be. Giving something your all will repeat great rewards. If you can't finish, don't start. Never go to bed angry at anyone. If you don't have something nice to say, don't say anything at all. Life is a mirror—smile at it. When everything seems against you, smile anyway. Live your life so you can look anyone in the eye.

BIRDIE ETCHISON, novelist

When my Australian grandmother came to visit, I was about five and my brother was a baby. She was changing his diaper and asked me to get a napkin. I went to the dining room and got one. Then she told me not to be "smart" and told me to get a napkin at once. We finally sorted it out—in Australia, a napkin is a diaper!

SHIRLEY STUELPNAGEL, needlework expert

A grandmother is rarely too busy or too tired to teach. Nana showed me how to knit, crochet, and make angel food cake. She paid me as much as ten dollars to learn a new piece for the piano—a lot of money in the 1940s!

Because she was a professional teacher, she considered every moment to be a rich opportunity for education. So she let her grandchildren mix chicken feed, recite poetry, cut with big scissors, practice striking safety matches, and use her sewing machine. And she taught them that living life with God was its own wonderful reward.

Recipe for Dry Skin

Combine one cup of oatmeal, a cup of water, two coffee spoons of good vanilla and about four spoons of baking soda. Mix up good and put in the water you use to wash your face and body.

NANNY STEWART

Recipe for Hair Lightening

(if the hair isn't too dark)

To lighten hair, use about a half-cup of chopped-up, newly pulled spring rhubarb to two cups of boiling water. Cool it off and strain through a fine sieve. After you wash your hair, rinse it in this rhubarb tea.

NANNY STEWART

I was born in 1887 and grew up on a big farm in Missouri. My mother worked hard all day, but she loved to spin on her maple spinning wheel. I think she would rather have been spinning than anything else in the world. I used to watch her toss the thread over the wheel when it was spun. She'd send me out in the horse-drawn sleigh with my father to deliver milk while the other kids were at school, and then she'd "rest" from her chores by spinning and singing hymns.

Women spin nowadays as a hobby, but we had to have the yarn and thread, and the cloth she wove, or we'd have had no clothes.

MABEL ADAMS, born 1887, died 1985.
Her oral history was given
on tape to Susan Betts.

A Grandmother's Memories

She puts her hands to the distaff,
and her hands hold the spindle.

Proverbs 31:19 *(NRSV)*

Recipe for Varnishing Chalk Pictures

To save a picture drawn in chalk or crayon on paper, brush it over with castor oil and let it dry. It will varnish the paper good, and you won't have a bad smell.

NANNY STEWART

From My Welsh Grandmother:

"Don't change clout til winter's out."
(Don't put away your long johns too early in the season; it's not healthy.)
MABEL TURNER, Connecticut

When grandmothers are missing from a society, that society loses its link to the wisdom of the past and the traditions that make the tribe able to reflect on itself. Grandmothers are civilization: They insist on things being done right, they defend the old ways, and they recall the language. Being a grandmother is a constant learning and teaching experience, because as grandmothers, women must learn to apply yesterday's wisdom to today's challenges.

Do not let your grandmother get old before you write down her recipes.

ANONYMOUS

Dr. Chase's Medical and Receipt Book (published in 1886) was a popular book for our grandmothers, sort of a *Betty Crocker's Cookbook* and a family medical book all rolled into one. Here's one favorite recipe from Dr. Chase. (One grandmother called this same recipe "head cake," because, she said, "It's so simple to remember, I can make it out of my head.")

Pound Cake

Ingredients: A pound of flour, a pound of butter, a pound of eggs, a pound of sugar. Beat together, add baking powder and salt, and bake in an oven that is not too hot.

Recipe for Stiff Kid Gloves

If your kid gloves are hard and stiff, put them on carefully, making sure you don't break any creases. Now pour a few drops of the finest olive oil in your palm and rub it all over both gloves, especially the fingers and thumbs. Use more oil if you need to. Then buff them dry with a very soft towel and wear them until they dry.

NANNY STEWART

The "New Look" arrived in 1947, while I was a senior in high school. We had still worn our short wartime skirts and long sloppy-joe sweaters with bobby socks and saddle shoes until that fall, when full skirts to the ankles, black or colored nylon hose, and "Gibson Girl" blouses became the rage. I wore the first Gibson blouse at my school: It had leg-o'-mutton sleeves and an inset yoke, with a small, flowing black bow at the neck.

My grandmother, who made it for me, said she'd made one just like it for herself—in 1900!

DOROTHY JOHNSON, born 1931

Recipe for White Hands

Keep a cut lemon on the washstand where you wash your hands. Every time you wash, rub them with the lemon before you dry them. Soon your hands will be whiter.

NONNY JOHNSON

Recipe for Keeping a Cat and Curing Hair Balls

When you get a new cat, every night for a week, butter its paws. The cat will lick it off and like you and stay there forever.

If your cat has hair balls, put Vaseline on its nose. It will lick it off and cure the hair balls.

NANNY STEWART

*I*t was with real anticipation and relish that you came into the room that held Grandma, and sat down on your little stool and folded your hands around your knees. For pretty soon Grandma would drop some remark—perhaps a very willful remark—and begin opening up her mind.

Just the same, I used to feel a little sorry for Alice and me then. We were like little plants that managed to maintain a foothold in a crannied wall, or like Arizona birds who must make their nests in a high cactus, not that it isn't prickly but that there is no other safety to be chosen. However interesting it was to live with Grandma, it was not easy.

Grandma Griswold was—well, what her neighbours called "different." Grandma purposed to be different in more ways than one, and, for her, differentness began at home. The amazing thing about Grandma's housekeeping was that, even to the close of the first quarter of the twentieth century, every utensil, every way of doing, was just as purely eighteenth century as Grandma could manage to keep it. She was ninety-six when she died in 1925, and throughout her life—almost a century long—Grandma held back "modern improvements"—you could hear the ironical quotation marks she always spoke into the phrase—from contaminating her home.

BERTHA DAMON,
Grandma Called It Carnal

Grandmother was in the parlor already: bending and leaning over the arm of a chair, she was standing at the wall and praying fervently. Papa stood near her. She turned around to us and smiled, when she noticed that we were hiding behind our backs the presents which we were to offer. . . .

"Well, do show us, Nikolenka! What is it you have, a box or a drawing?" said Papa to me. There was nothing to be done; with a trembling hand I gave her the crushed, fatal roll; but my voice refused to serve me, and I stopped silent before Grandmother. I was beside myself, thinking that, instead of the expected drawing, they would read aloud my worthless poem. How am I to tell the agony through which I passed, when Grandmother began to read my poem; when, unable to make it out, she stopped in the middle of the verse in order to look at Papa with a smile, which then seemed to me to be one of mockery; and when, her eyes being weak, she did not finish reading it, but handed it to Papa and asked him to read it from the beginning? It seemed to me that she did so because she was tired of reading such horrible and badly scrawled verses. . . . I was waiting for him to snap my nose with the poem. . . . But nothing of the sort happened; on the contrary, after it had been read, Grandmother said: "Charmant!" and kissed my brow.

"Childhood, "
from *Complete Works of Count Tolstoy*

Wisdom's Love and Affirmation

She openeth her mouth with wisdom;
and in her tongue is the law of kindness.

Proverbs 31:26

Grandmother Faber's
Little German Love Song

Gramma Faber, a tall, stately, ample lady, came from Germany when she was seven, but she never forgot her country's songs. I especially remember one she taught me as I sat in her lap: "Du, du liegst mir am Herzen" or "You, You Are in My Heart Always."

A few years later—in 1939—I sang it to my first grade class at Sprague Grammar School in Waterville, Connecticut. My teacher must have thought it was worth sharing because she led me into a nearby classroom where I was asked to share the song with the children in that grade also. So I sang, "Du, du liegst mir am Herzen."

Her little song, lovingly taught from a grandmother's heart and embedded in my young one, must have prepared me to have an open heart to receive the Savior. And perhaps her song is the reason I call my poems "heart word art."

Yes, Gramma Faber, you were very wise—you sang into me again and again, a little melody of heart-love. . .and I have been living and singing heart-songs ever since. The strange thing is, Gramma, I didn't really know what the German words meant until sixty years later, in 1999.

DAVID ALAN FABER, poet

*Kind words can be short
and easy to speak,
but their echoes are truly endless.*

MOTHER TERESA

Wise grandmothers regret nothing that ever happened to them, because they know that in anguish they grew, in joy they flowered, and in sorrow they learned appreciation. We turn to Grandmother trusting that she will help us find answers, show us beauty and wonder, and call us to full personhood. She not only knows what we do not know; she also is wise enough to take time with us until we learn it. No other woman can make a child feel so handsome, so clever, so skillful, so loved, as a grandmother.

randma Gypsy never learned how to drive, so her Methodist husband would drive her to the Southern Baptist church and sit in the parking lot.

She was about four-feet-eight, with arthritic fingers and toes, but wonderful blue eyes. She had an infectious laugh and loved to tell stories, mostly about my dad who had been a handful as a child. She claimed that her family could trace its roots to royalty, a certain Reynolds castle in Germany. She really was named Gypsy and was born somewhere in Kentucky. She had three sisters: Trixie, Mamie, and Catherine.

Even though one of my arms was paralyzed from polio in infancy, she taught me how to roll dough and make her lemon pie, which I always thought was heavenly. Once when I had no one to help me take the pie from the oven, I tried to do it with one hand. Of course I overturned it and it fell in a heap. We ate it anyway and called it "heavenly hash."

Why Do I Love My Grandmother? Let Me Count the Ways.

She used to take me to garage sales every weekend; she might not have thought it was a big deal, but I still reminisce every time I see a garage sale. I remember when she bought me a Snoopy pillowcase.

I remember watching three very important newscasts at my grandmother's house: the fall of the Berlin Wall, the student protest in Tienanmen Square, and the San Francisco earthquake.

I remember Christmases at her house, a goat named Sara, ducks, and a gigantic backyard, big enough for my friend and me to get lost in.

When she bought her new car, she came to our house when I was playing basketball in the driveway. She immediately took me for a ride and played a cassette of Paul Simon's *Graceland,* and every time I hear it I think about that evening.

Best of all, she flew 3,000 miles to see the miracle of my life, my daughter Emyle, when she was born October 13, 1998.

ANDY BETTS
(father of the author's only great-grandchild)

*M*y grandmother came to the U.S. as an immigrant from Norway. I don't think it was her idea, because she never wanted to speak English—and never did. I learned to speak Norwegian because that's all anyone spoke around her. She was beautiful, soft in all the right places where grandmoms should be, so when she held me it was like lying on a warm pillow that hugged you back. She was the best cook in the world and made us all the wonderful desserts and special dishes from the old country.

Her wisdom was expressed as love. Whenever I stayed with them, which was often while my father was in the service, and later the TB sanitarium, Mom (we all called her that though I pronounced it "Mum") and my grandfather would welcome me into their bed in the cold North Dakota mornings. I would snuggle down between them feeling loved and special. "Mom" had thirteen children but she never ran out of hugs.

PATRICIA RUSHFORD, psychotherapist and mystery novelist

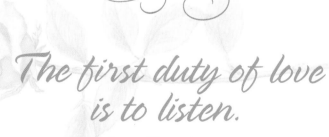

The first duty of love is to listen.

PAUL TILLICH

Most grandmothers touch a lot.
They hug, they stroke,
they pat, and they cuddle.
Even after we're grown
they find ways to
run their hands over our backs
or ruffle our hair.
Somehow, although they may have
as many irons in the fire as parents do,
they find more time to make
physical contact with their grandchildren;
and the grandchildren never forget.

Once when I said I would never get married, my grandmother smiled wisely and told me I'd be married as soon as I turned eighteen. She was right. She was loving, wise, and a staunch ally for me. When I think of her now, I think one word: Love.

LINDA SHANDS,
rancher and author

Grandma Brown kept cookie bars in large Folger's coffee cans tucked away in the back of her freezer. When company came to visit, out came a can or two, filled with butterscotch and chocolate chip cookie bars. I remember waiting impatiently for them to thaw; she apparently knew exactly when they reached melt-in-your-mouth temperature. I'd watch as she placed a paper lace doily on a china plate painted with orange blossoms. She'd arrange the cookie bars in a decorative circle, then hand the plate to me. Together we'd go into the living room, and as she passed out pretty paper napkins, I'd present the plate of cookies. After the cookies were served, she would pour coffee. Handing the delicate cup and saucer to me, she'd patiently instruct me on how to carry and present the steaming cup without spilling.

"Take small steps, and keep your chin up," she'd say. I'd carry the cups slowly, my head held high. In Grandma's house, I wasn't a clumsy teenager, the bull in a china closet, my father called me. I was a young lady, able to pass coffee and cookies with grace and ease.

JOY THOMPSON

My grandmother was my refuge. No matter how miserable I was at home, I always brightened up with her. I loved going to her house Friday nights for supper. When I was coming she cooked up a storm. She began cooking at six o'clock in the morning—potato pancakes, chicken soup, and boiled chicken. After dinner she would take me into the candy store and make a big malted milk and urge ice cream cones on me. "Julie, aren't you hungry yet?" she would ask me every half hour.

"Julie,"
My Nights and Days

Grandma lived with my family for about ten years, and she was so wise in the way she treated me that I didn't have to talk about school or feel that I had to please her; she was just there and she loved me. Her big room was a sanctuary.

I have learned even more about her since she died. But none of that seems as important as the quiet sharing we had when she lived with us.

LUCY STRANDLIEN,
musician

The Language of Flowers

Our grandmothers and great-grandmothers had a symbolic vocabulary for expressing their love, a vocabulary of flowers that we have lost today. Flowers, a beautiful part of creation, expressed love; they were tributes of affection, honor, valor, and fame. Here is our grandmothers' language of flowers:

Acacia: concealed love
Adonis vernalia: bitter memories
Azalea: romance
Bachelors' button: hope in love
Barberry: sharpness; satire
Basil: hatred
Camellia: pity
Cedar: "I live for thee"

Cypress with marigold: despair
Dahlia: forever thine
Daisy: Michaelmas, farewell
Dogwood flower: "Am I
   indifferent to you?"
Eglantine rose: "I wound to heal"
Elm: dignity
Evening primrose: inconstancy
Forget-me-not: true love
Foxglove: insincerity
Gardenia: transport; ecstasy
Geranium, ivy: "Your hand for
   the next dance"
Guelder rose (snowball): writer
Heather: solitude
Holly: foresight
Hyacinth: jealousy
Ice plant: "Your looks freeze me"
Iris: message

Ivy: matrimony
Jonquil: "Return my affection"
Judas tree flower: betrayed
Juniper: perfect loveliness
Kalmia: treachery
Kennedia: intellectual beauty
Lady's slipper: capricious beauty
Lavender: distrust
Lettuce: coldhearted
Magnolia: peerless and proud
Maple: reserve
Marigold: cruelty
Mullen: good nature
Mushroom: suspicion
Narcissus: egotism
Nasturtium: patriotism
Nightshade: bitter truth
Oak: hospitality
Oleander: "Beware"
Oats: music
Orange: generosity
Pansy: "Think of me"
Peony: anger
Phlox: "Our souls are united"
Poppy: consolation
Quince: temptation

Rose: beauty
Rose, yellow: decrease of love
Rosemary: "Your presence
    revives me"
Rue: disdain
Saffron: "Excess is dangerous"
Snapdragon: presumption
St. John's wort: superstition
Tansy: "I declare against you"
Tea rose: always lovely
Thistle: austerity
Tulip: declaration of love
Valerian: accommodating
    disposition
Violet, blue: love
Violet, white: modesty
Weeping willow: forsaken
Wheat: prosperity
Wormwood: absence
Yarrow: cure for heartache
Yew: sorrow
Zinnia: absent friends

from *The Rules of Etiquette
and Home Culture,*
by R. HOUGHTON

A Grandmother's home
always bids
WELCOME

Wisdom's Mercy

Let not mercy and truth forsake thee:
bind them about thy neck;
write them upon the table of thine heart.

Proverbs 3:3

Unless we learn the meaning of mercy, we will never have any real knowledge of what it means to love Christ.

THOMAS MERTON

Do wise grandmothers ever show anger? Yes, at injustice, or cruelty, or betrayal of trust. But they are long-suffering and patient with unruliness, silliness, failure, and even untruthfulness. A woman who has lived long enough to have two generations of descendants has also experienced, and learned to give, mercy. Showing mercy may, in fact, be the major mark of wisdom.

Who is as sympathetic as a grandmother? She kisses hurts when we're tiny and hugs us in the middle of teenage tantrums. She takes in stray children who cannot live with their parents, and rears them "in the fear of the Lord." She races to school to pick up a sick grandchild and knows the arcane secrets of milk toast or chamomile tea. When parents think their children deserve punishment, she urges mercy. And when everyone else has forgotten, a grandmother prays for her grandchildren.

God tempers the wind to the shorn lamb.

Proverb from an English grandmother

"I don't know, grandmother," said the princess, beginning to cry. "I can't always do myself as I should like. And I don't always try. I'm very sorry anyhow."

The lady stooped, lifted her in her arms, and sat down with her in her chair, holding her close to her bosom.

GEORGE MACDONALD,
The Princess and the Goblin

Blessed are the merciful: for they shall obtain mercy.

Matthew 5:7

*T*each me to feel another's woe,
To hide the faults I see;
That mercy I to others show
That mercy shown to me.

ALEXANDER POPE

Let my children be committed to Thy mercy.

KATHERINE VON BORA, 1540

*V*ery little shocks grandmothers. Their wisdom is born out of experience. They've lived through many presidents and sometimes several wars; they have seen the dollar rise and fall, worshiped with a score of pastors, made dozens of friends and lost a few, given birth, faced death, given loved ones back to God, rocked screaming colicky infants, nursed aging parents, and fought lovingly with husbands. They remember fashions of another era and smile when those styles return. Their Bibles are often well-thumbed and their mirrors often give them back an image of wise, loving patience.

He that followeth after righteousness and mercy findeth life, righteousness, and honour.

Proverbs 21:21

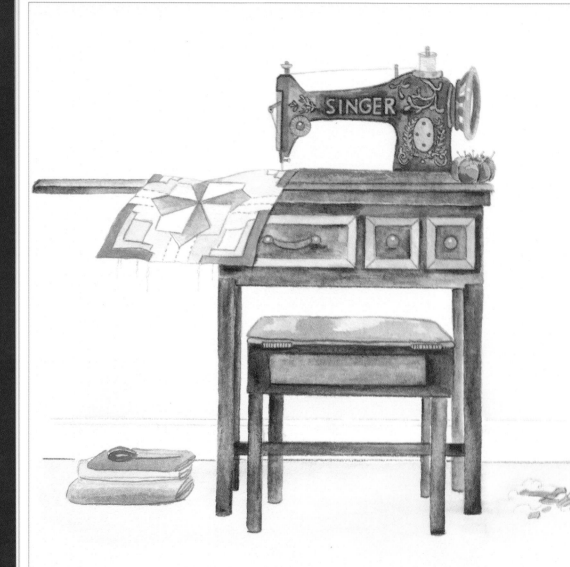

Wisdom's Joy and Beauty

The king's daughter is
all glorious within: her clothing is
of wrought gold.

Psalm 45:13

*M*y grandmother, bless her big German heart, was a contest enthusiast. Together we won a real "Lassie" collie from the first *Lassie* TV show, we made two television commercials with Tom Posten, and we won my own Annie Oakley six-guns. Her wisdom was in her passion for living.

JOANIE JAGODA, layout artist

"*H*ow old are you?"
"Ten," answered Tangle.
"You don't look it," said the lady.
"How old are you, please?" returned Tangle.
"Thousands of years old," answered the lady.
"You don't look like it," said Tangle.
"Don't I? I think I do. Don't you see how beautiful I am?"
. . . "And what is your name, please?" asked Tangle.
"Grandmother," answered the lady.

GEORGE MACDONALD (1824-1905),
The Golden Key

The fairest garden
in her looks,
And in her mind
the wisest books.

ABRAHAM COWLEY (1618-1667), *The Garden*

The Family is the Country of the heart. There is an angel in the Family who, by the mysterious influence of grace, of sweetness, and of love, renders the fulfillment of duties less wearisome, sorrows less bitter. The only pure joys unmixed with sadness which it is given to man to taste upon earth are, thanks to this angel, the joys of the Family.

GIUSEPPE MAZZINI, 1805–1872

Women with a high sense of well-being have suffered just as many hardships as their most miserable contemporaries report. They describe the same disappointments in husbands and children, the same losses of jobs, homes, money, dreams, and yet they feel positive about their lives.

The critical difference is this: They have usually confronted a difficulty, rocked a boat, picked themselves up, and taken the painful steps necessary to free themselves from what they finally perceived as a trap, self-made or imposed. This sort of change is the source of a good part of the euphoria among the happiest women.

Putting it in the simplest terms, by middle age, you know better than at any prior stage who you are, what you need, and how to get it.

GAIL SHEEHY, *Pathfinders*

But thy eternal Summer shall not fade,
Nor lose possession of that fair thou owest;
Nor shall Death brag thou wanderest in his shade,
When in eternal lines to time thou growest:
So long as men can breathe, or eyes can see,
So long lives this, and this gives life to thee.

WILLIAM SHAKESPEARE,
"Shall I Compare Thee to a Summer's Day?"

*Charm is deceitful, and beauty
is vain, but a woman
who fears the LORD
is to be praised.*

Proverbs 31:30 (NRSV)

He that raises a large family does, indeed, while he lives to observe them, stand a broader mark for sorrow; but then he stands a broader mark for pleasure too.

BENJAMIN FRANKLIN

Wisdom's Strength

Strength and honour
are her clothing.

Proverbs 31:25

*N*avajos confer great honor on a woman of any age by calling her "Grandmother." A grandmother is a wise woman of stature in the tribal community. Because the inheritance system among Navajos is matrilineal—that is, the wealth passes through the mothers—the grandmother is a chief elder in her clan. She holds the keys to knowledge: She has always known how to shear a sheep, weave a rug, stop a child's tears, tame an angry, drinking man, cook a stew for forty people, wash a girl's hair in yucca suds for her womanhood rites, and drive a truck over the mountains.

Nowadays Navajo grandmothers become doctors and lawyers. They cure cancers, program computers, carry briefcases, and lobby the government. But they are above all still respected as the source of tribal wisdom.

*M*y wonderful grandmother taught cooking to the Navajo boarding students at Keams Canyon, Arizona. She was a fluent Navajo speaker, having grown up in New Mexico, a talented amateur sculptor and painter, and when she was in her late fifties, she was made a member of the Diné, or Navajo nation.

She taught me how to make a lemon meringue pie, to bind a book with fabric, and to speak some Navajo. But more importantly, she showed me I could dare to reach beyond ordinary life, to respect people of all shapes and colors, and to be as creative as possible. I loved her for her wild spirit and her tender mercy.

The Mexican word for grand-mother is *la abuela*. Because many parents in Mexico have to work in fields or factories, *la abuela* is frequently the one who cares for the children. Her daily routine will begin when she rises early to sweep the porch, water the plants that hang there in clay pots, and sweep the yard, which usually doesn't have a lawn. Then she makes the tortillas, grinding the corn in a stone *metate,* or trudging with the children to the

A Grandmother spreads sunshine wherever she goes...

groceria for *masa,* corn flour. She pats a ball of the masa dough between her hands until it becomes a tortilla, then tosses it on a hot pan or griddle, teaching the children so say, "Tortillitas, Pa-pa-pa, Tortillitas, Ma-ma-ma"—the Mexican version of patty-cake. She may cook as many as fifty tortillas in a morning, because they are the "staff of life" for that society.

For a treat she gives the children *panocha*—a brown sugar candy —or dark red, translucent squash candy. She washes their clothes by hand, in as little water as possible, for if she lives outside Mexico's bigger cities, chances are good that she has to carry the water for as much as a mile.

La abuela is always known as a wise woman who is just and merciful. She is at the center of Mexican society and the men of her family go to her for wisdom. She is a strong woman.

$\mathcal{M}$imi was Pennsylvania Dutch, and to me like someone from a different land, a different time. I loved her softness, her ability to look at me when she talked to me and let me feel her love. Everything about her was different from me; she was from a different culture and still that was my culture too. I was fascinated by her difference, yet the connection between us was strong. She made the connection and poured her wisdom into it. Mimi was the one who made me realize that I wasn't a product of the present, but part of generations of others—and that connection made me stronger.

SUSAN BETTS, seminarian

$\mathcal{I}$f I didn't start painting, I would have raised chickens. I could still do it now. I would never sit back in a rocking chair, waiting for someone to help me. I have often said, before I would call for help from outsiders, I would rent a room in the city some place and give pancake suppers, just pancakes and syrup, and they could have water, like a little breakfast. I never dreamed that the pictures would bring in so much, and as for all that publicity, and as for the fame which came to Grandma so late, that I am too old to care for now. . . . I felt older when I was sixteen than I ever did since. I was old and sedate when I left the Whitesides, I suppose it was the life I led, I had to be so ladylike. Even now I am not old, I never think of it, yet I am a grandmother to eleven grandchildren, I also have seventeen great-grandchildren, that's a plenty!

GRANDMA MOSES, *My Life History*

My grandmother died at ninety-six, and for most of her life, she was physically very active. When she was sixty-five, she could beat my brother and me in a foot race. She didn't retire from private nursing until she was eighty-five. She used to pasture her cows in the morning, then go bring them down at night, often riding the last cow home. She had a vegetable garden until she was ninety-three.

I told her everything, from the time I was four until she died. Her sense of justice was perfect, her wisdom absolute, and her humor unfailing.

RONALD INGRAM,
engineering consultant

But joy is wisdom, time an endless song.

WILLIAM BUTLER YEATS,
"Land of Heart's Desire"

*C*ynthia Jane Reel Smith was an independent woman. She lived across the street from the high school I attended, and I frequently spent time at her house. My memories of her are of a strong woman who had control of her destiny.

Her walls were covered with her original paintings that were in various stages of creation. She also had a basket of stereopticon slides and a viewer. They were the springboard for telling me stories of her early life growing up in Eastern Oregon.

She was always interesting. She had owned timberland in Eastern Oregon (in her own name). To buy the lumber for the house that my grandfather built in 1900, she had earned money through her photography. She bought a tourist hotel on the northwest coast and ran it until her health became poor. After having a kidney removed, she and Grandpa bought property with a greenhouse. When Grandpa died she earned money by selling paintings and making agate jewelry for the tourist trade.

I really believe that her independence and her creativity contributed to who I am, and to my feelings that a woman can be independent. She taught me that a woman can control her own life, but concern and consideration of others is equally important.

EMILY MORRIS, retired

My grandmother is three hundred feet tall and walks on balloons. Her knowledge is as vast as time: She has answers for any question I ask. Her best friend is Jesus Himself, and to call His name is, for her, to travel to heaven. She lives with zeal as she goes, her joy is infectious, her wild curly hair corners the face that writes experience. Wise as any, she truly runs with the wolves.

ADAM,
student at University of Nebraska

My grandmothers were strong.
They followed plows and bent to toil.
They moved through fields
sowing seed.
They touched earth and grain grew.
They were full of sturdiness
and singing.

MARGARET WALKER, "Lineage,"
Grandparents' Houses

*S*ome types of lumber do not have structural integrity or the fiber necessary to hold a load without breaking. Heartwood—the core of the tree, the dense inner rings that give a tree backbone so it can sway in the wind without breaking—is the sturdiest. . . . True heartwood is difficult to find these days. . .

Childhood is like the heartwood—the strong center close to the foundation of our lives, always there. We are undeniably the products of our homes. . . . To truly appreciate the gift of your life, you must consider your heartwood—the original material with which you began. . .

NANCIE CARMICHAEL,
Your Life, God's Home

*J*uly 5th, 1868: Today I have completed sixty-four Springtimes. . . And now here I am, a very old woman, embarked on my sixty-fifth year. By one of those strange oddities in my destiny, I am now in much better health, much stronger, much more active, than I ever was in my youth. . . . I am troubled by no hankering after the days of my youth: I am no longer ambitious for fame; I desire no money except insofar as I should like to be able to leave something to my children and grandchildren. . . . This astonishing old age. . .has brought me neither infirmity nor lowered vitality.

Can I still make myself useful? That one may legitimately ask, and I think that I can answer "yes." I feel that I may be useful in a more personal, more direct way than ever before. I have, though how I do not know, acquired much wisdom. I am better equipped to bring up children. . . . It is quite wrong to think of old age as a downward slope. One climbs higher and higher with the advancing, and that, too, with surprising strides.

How good life is when all that one loves is aswarm with life!

GEORGE SAND,
quoted by André Maurois in
Lélia, The Life of George Sand

Wisdom's Bounty

The righteous shall flourish like the palm tree:
he shall grow like a cedar in Lebanon.
Those that be planted in the house of the LORD
shall flourish in the courts of our God.
They shall still bring forth fruit in old age;
they shall be fat and flourishing.

Psalm 92:12–14

Grandmere's New Orleans Calais

To a cup of cooked white rice, add a mashed cake of yeast, an egg, and a cup of flour and stir very gently. Let this rise overnight. In the morning for breakfast, drop by spoonfuls into very hot fat. As soon as the balls are golden, take them out, drain them on a clean napkin, and roll in sugar.

You can eat them hot or save them for noonday and eat them cold.

MADELEINE CHUMAINE, birthdate unknown

Grandchildren are the crown of the aged.

Proverbs 17:6 (NRSV)

*N*o one could make biscuits or corn bread like Grandmother made on that wood stove, and I can't remember ever going to her house but what there were biscuits and homemade jelly on  the table. I loved her homemade dumplings—she called them slipaways because you couldn't pick more than one up at a time or they would slip off your fork. I'll see her again someday and when I do the first thing I'll ask is, "Grandma, got any biscuits?"

B. POTTER

Gran Owen's Maryland Fried Chicken

*D*ip each piece of chicken in flour so it is white. Then dip it in a batter made of a cup of buttermilk, a beaten egg, about a cup of flour and a teaspoon of baking powder. Drop it into sizzling lard and then turn it down and cover for about fifteen minutes. Turn it over careful so you don't lose the juice. Cook uncovered for about fifteen more minutes. Use some leftover coating to thicken a good buttermilk gravy.

MAUDE OWEN, born 1880

What I bless my grandmother's memory for is that she sent Christmas packages every year from her home in Victoria, B.C., to us, her grandchildren in Oregon. Not unusual? It was in our house. Our father, a pastor in a strict Christian denomination, wouldn't allow us to celebrate Christmas or to have a Christmas tree or to exchange presents in the home (Christmas being a pagan celebration that Christians had no business observing); so you can see what a blessing Granny Price was. That brave woman didn't give a fig for my father's idiosyncratic view. Her grandkids were going to have presents for Christmas.

THE REVEREND JONATHAN WELDON

Over the river, and through the woods,
    to Grandmother's house we go;
the horse knows the way to carry the sleigh
    through white and drifted snow.
Over the river and through the woods,
    now Grandmother's cap I spy!
Hurrah for the fun, Is the pudding done?
    Hurrah for the pumpkin pie.

AUTHOR UNKNOWN

Nana's
Southern Pecan Pralines

Measure out a cup each of brown sugar and white sugar, and add a cup of light cream.

Put into a thick, heavy saucepan and very slowly cook up to a medium ball stage. Stir in a half cup of chopped pecans. Pour out in circles on buttered waxed paper and press in pecan halves. After these harden, put them in waxed sandwich bags and tie with red Christmas ribbon.

ELIZABETH BLANCHE STEPHENS, born 1883

Baba Nicolov's Szelnick

Make a strudel or filo pastry so thin you can read a newspaper through it. Lay down a sheet, oil it good with melted butter, and cover with another sheet. Do this for five sheets and lay in a cookie pan. This is the bottom. Make the top the same way. Here is the filling: Stir up two cups of hoop cheese or cottage cheese, four eggs, a teaspoon of good olive oil and a sprinkle of salt and pepper. Spread it over the bottom and put the top on. Bake about twenty minutes with the firebox not too hot. Cool it off and cut it in squares. This is a wonderful meal for any day.

ANA NICOLOV, born in Macedonia around 1889

My father's mother was a wonderful cook and wise enough to know families should eat together. My mouth waters even now, remembering the spiraling mound of mashed potatoes in the golden bowl she always served them in, along with rich roast gravy to ladle over them. Big family get-togethers with lots of laughter around the table made her a happy woman and kept me coming back for the cookies that were always available in her kitchen.

BOBBIE CHRISTENSEN, school librarian

Salt Fish and Potato

1-2 pieces salt fish, cooked (and crumbled to look for bones)
1-2 potatoes, mashed (depending on amount of fish)
36 tbsps. salad dressing
¼-½ c. oil (depending on amount of fish and potatoes)
Nutmeg

Blend or mix all ingredients. Mixture will be very thick. Serve with thin crackers, such as onion thins. No one will believe that it contains salt fish and potatoes!

PAULINE TARRANT, a Newfoundland grandmother

Bubby's Matzoh Ball Soup

Make a good boiling broth from Kosher chicken

5 cups corn meal
1 cup self-rising flour
    (add 1 tsp. of baking powder if not self-rising flour)
½ cup dried Kosher chicken
1 dozen eggs
2 handfuls dried parsley, the stems cut off
½ handful rosemary
2 cloves garlic, pulverized
32 ozs. peanut oil

Combine above ingredients. If you're making this outside as Bubby did, the bowl was covered and placed in cold water. Otherwise put in refrigerator 20 minutes or until oil sets. Matzoh balls are rolled into the size of golf balls. They will swell to 4 times their size.

   Cook 20 minutes in the boiling chicken broth. Make sure each person gets one or two balls in their soup.

Grandmother, you gave me the wealth of detail.
You taught me to love grass and moss, ants
and butterflies. . . .You gave me my first trees and my first
sunset, mushroom hunts and the bliss of long walks.
E. M. ALMEDINGEN, "Gifts From My Grandmother,"
Grandparents' Houses

It was a Christmas morning during the Great Depression, and I had received more gifts than many of the children in my town did: a teddy bear, a furnished doll house, two dolls, and several games. My mother and grandmother were in the kitchen, preparing a feast of both turkey and ham when a man came to the door, asking for my father. They went out together and when Father came back, he was white with shock. He told us one of the workers at the town mine had asked for help, and taken them to his tiny adobe shack, where seventeen people, all his relatives from Mexico, lived in one room: They included a starving mother trying in vain to nurse an infant, and two very old ladies.

My grandmother looked at Father with her china-blue eyes and said, "Frank, get a big box." She began loading the turkey, the ham, several bottles of milk—just delivered that morning—and all the dinner accompaniments into boxes, which Father took to the poor family.

We had canned beans and lunch meat sandwiches for Christmas dinner. They tasted like bread from heaven, because the house was overflowing with my grandmother's love.

*A*lwyn's grandmother sat in the sitting room only when there were guests, or when, by the south window, she held the *Milwaukee Sentinel* or the *Christian Herald* on a level with the ridge of her old-fashioned corset, discovering what went on in the world through her unsuitably small spectacles. Her life, like that of primitive women, revolved about the place where food was prepared. Her thoughts and even her recollections were accessory to whatever she was doing at the moment; they resembled her habit of whispering to herself, often with vehemence, while she worked. So it was in the kitchen, her broad lap full of pea pods or stockings to be darned, with one eye on a simmering kettle or the bread rising in pans, that she was most likely to satisfy her grandson's curiosity. Sometimes she replied to questions which he was too young to ask with obscure allusions or partial avowals, which, like the rays of a magic lantern, illuminated with disconnected pictures the darkness of many lives—in fact, the darkness of life itself.

GLENWAY WESTCOTT,
The Grandmothers, a Family Portrait

She opens her hand
to the poor, and reaches
out her hands
to the needy.

Proverbs 31:20 (NRSV)

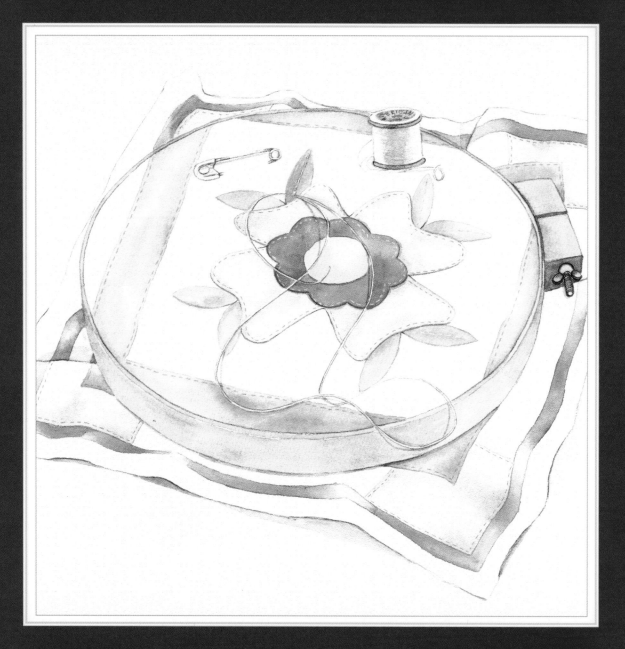

Grandmothers
of the Heart

The aged women likewise,
that they be in behaviour as becometh holiness,
not false accusers, not given to much wine,
teachers of good things;
That they may teach the young women to be sober,
to love their husbands, to love their children.

Titus 2:3–4

Any Woman Can Be a Grandmother

"*L*et us all go to Viamede for the winter," suggested his mother. Would that not suit you. . . ?"

"Suppose you go in relays," suggested Chester.

"Why not say we, instead of you, Brother Chester," laughed Elsie Raymond. "I'm sure Grandma included you in her invitation."

"Certainly," said Grandma Elsie, giving Chester one of her sweet smiles. "May I not count you and Lucilla among my grandchildren?"

MARTHA FINLEY, *Elsie [Dinsmore] and Her Namesakes*

To walk with God takes courage, and in old age God asks us to walk with Him.

JOHN LA FARGE, *Reflections on Growing Old*

A Substitute Grandmother

I fought a running skirmish with Mrs. Olive Bird, my stern, unbending, seldom-smiling high school English and typing teacher—and lifelong wisdom figure. Years later in times that test conscience and character, I recognize that her subtle lessons still guide me. When I realized her influence, it was too late to thank her directly, but I think of her often and know in my heart that she smiles.

MAURICE VAN, artist

Wisdom is that olive that springeth from the heart, bloometh on the tongue, and beareth fruit in the actions.

ELIZABETH GRYMESTOM,
Miscellanea—Meditations, 1604

I had a shortage of real grandmothers. There was, however, a lady in her 70s who was the pianist for our Sunday school and our community poet-in-residence. She gave me free piano lessons, but the other things she taught me were more important. After my weekly lesson, we talked about everything: history (her father had been one of the original surveyors of the Oregon and southwest Washington areas for mapmaking), and geography (she had been born in Penzance, England, and had crossed the U.S. in a covered wagon), and the secret of basic poetry construction. For the first time in my life I realized normal people could make poems, music, and books. She was my good friend, and the nearest thing to a grandmother I had.

ELSIE LARSON, novelist

American Sign Language for "Grandmother"

*T*he sign for "grandmother" is made by touching your chin with the thumb of your right hand, as when signing "mother." The hand should be open. Now, move your hand forward in two small arches.

*All wisdom
may be
reduced to
two words—
wait and hope.*
ALEXANDER DUMAS

The care of the old for the young is no different from the care of the young for the old. Real care takes place when we are no longer separated by the walls of fear, but have found each other on the common ground of the human condition, which is mortal, but, therefore, very very precious.

HENRI NOUWEN,
Aging: The Fulfillment of Life

Grandmothers in Heaven

Wherefore seeing we also are compassed about
with so great a cloud of witnesses,
let us lay aside every weight,
and the sin which doth so easily beset us,
and let us run with patience the race
that is set before us.

Hebrews 12:1

The death of a grandmother
is the end of a time in life.
Sometimes one never finds
another confidante
so trustworthy or another judge
so fair.
Life without that ancestress
is a little reduced:
At her funeral
the flowers may look pale
alongside her memory.

My mother's mother was very very short and very very wide. I remember her kitchen with its worn but spotless linoleum, and I always went in through the kitchen door. She always had an apron on and I couldn't get two steps inside without being hugged to death and smothered with Grandma's kisses.

I remember most the last time we went in through the kitchen. Aunts and uncles were there, but everything was quiet. We had been out for a drive and decided to just stop by unannounced. We walked into the kitchen and my mother started to sob, then cry, and cry louder. Soon, there was a room full of women crying. I couldn't figure out what had happened, but where was Grandma? She never missed out on hugging me.

I found out Grandma had died that morning while hanging wash out to dry in her front yard. I have one strong memory of her: She liked me best. And every other grandchild in the family thought the same thing.

GEORGE BETTS, systems analyst

I sincerely believe Grandma was my Guardian Angel on Earth and is now watching over me from above. I am a better person for knowing June Murphy and for having her love.

DEBBIE ROGERS

We understood
Her by her sight; her pure and eloquent blood
Spoke in her cheeks, and so distinctly wrought
That one might almost say her body thought.

JOHN DONNE, *Funeral Elegies,*
"On the Death of Mistress Drury"

Grandma had fair, almost translucent skin. Even when she'd wear a *babushka,* the word used for scarf in her native Slovakia, her face was lovely and represented wisdom to me.

Having my hands washed by Grandma was an experience. Grandma would take my two hands in hers, and as the warm water flowed, she would gently wash my hands with Camay soap. Somehow, the combination of her loving, squeezing motion on my two little hands, while she talked to me, saying my name in Slovak, left a memory. In her wisdom, she must have known that her touch would leave an imprint on my life.

Grandma loved God, and she was a peacemaker. When two people were arguing, she would say, "Step aside. One person cannot argue by himself."

Grandma died when I was sixteen. Now I'm a mother of four children. The other night I had a dream of Grandma. Her eyes were as blue as I remember them to be. In my dream, I asked her to pray for each of my children as I named them one by one. She smiled and said she would, then she turned and walked back to heaven. When I awoke, I realized to what degree my grandmother had made an impact on my life. Somewhere in my heart, I still needed her.

KATHLEEN RUCKMAN, religious writer

To rest in God
eternally is
the supreme joy
of Heaven.

BEDE JARRETT

In my Father's house
are many mansions:
if it were not so,
I would have told you.
I go to prepare a place
for you.

John 14:2

Seeing God in Grandma's Face

And Mary said,
My soul doth magnify the Lord,
and my spirit hath rejoiced
in God my Saviour.

Luke 1:46–47

*I*t isn't at the moment a woman becomes a grandmother that wisdom descends on her. What makes her wise is her years of living, her struggle to be whole, her successes in being human, her experiences of love and grace as her children grow up and make mistakes, the losses she suffers, and the joys she revels in. A true grandmother knows when to guide and when to stand aside, and she is always available but never intrusive. And grandmothers are very often a child's first real connection to God.

Life's Lessons

I learn, as the years roll onward
And leave the past behind
That much I had counted sorrow
But proves that God is kind;
That many a flower I had longed for
Had hidden a thorn of pain,
And many a rugged bypath
Led to fields of ripened grain.

AUTHOR UNKNOWN

*M*other was busy with our large family, but Gran was my friend. She lived with us and read a chapter of both the Old and New Testament every night. She corrected us according to the Bible, when she reckoned we needed it, and prayed for all of us.

I had an eye problem and didn't read aloud very well, so one year during summer vacation, she was wise enough to have me read a chapter of the Bible to her every night!

ELWYN LARSON, retired

"*W*hy can't we see Charley any more?" asked Dotty, peering anxiously into the sky.

"I don't know exactly why," replied Prudy, "but Grandma Read said God doesn't wish it. He has put a seal over our eyes, so an angel could stand before us and we wouldn't know it."

"Ah!" said Dotty in a low voice; and though she could see nothing, it seemed to her the air was full of angels.

SOPHIE MAY,
Dotty Dimple at Her Grandmother's

God sees us with not only a father's knowing eyes or a father's hopes and dreams, but with that careening joy that grandparents pour onto their grandchildren.

As Andrew disrupts my Mary meditation and smears my Martha blue jeans with applesauce, I hold him at arm's length and threaten to do violence to his person if he doesn't stay out of the dog's water; and in the middle of this chastening, I hug him in the throes of overwhelming love.

"God is a grandmother," I say into Andrew's warm, powdered neck, and he holds on for all he is worth, which is considerable. God is a grandmother because God has that ridiculously unconditional love for us. Even as He hastens and chastens His will to make own, He holds my wriggling and sinful soul away from Him, and His love comes pouring down from the throne.

KRISTEN JOHNSON INGRAM,
With the Huckleberry Christ

I didn't understand that my grandmother had wisdom to impart to me until I was about ten. She owned an antique shop full of lovely exotic things. I spent the summer of my tenth year attending a morning program at the downtown YMCA in Richmond, Virginia, and the afternoons at my grandmother's shop. The shop was bright in the front where the windows let in the hot summer sun. As you went to the back of the narrow four-story building, the gloom was cooler and inviting. The tables were covered with candy dishes, cups and saucers, cut glass, bed warmers, salt sellers and china figurines.

In the gloom of the middle of the shop, paintings from around the world hung on the walls. One from Japan depicted the Nativity. There was Mary, Joseph, the Baby Jesus, and peasants. There were even three very large men, in rich ceremonial robes that looked like Samurai. I supposed the three represented the Wise Men. I started laughing and told my grandmother, "Look, this Japanese painting has Baby Jesus all wrong. They've made him Japanese. Everybody knows that's not right."

"Well, Missy, what does Jesus look like?"

"Grandma, everybody knows what Jesus looks like. He looks just like us."

"Yes, child, that's just what the Japanese think."

What a revolutionary idea! I started to ask what did Jesus really look like, what was the truth of the matter. The look on my grandmother's face stopped those words before they could be spoken. She had told me the truth of the matter: Jesus looks like us, all of us.

NANCY GALLAGHER, accountant

Grace means God accepts me just as I am. He does not require or insist that I measure up to someone else's standard of performance. He loves me completely, thoroughly, and perfectly. There's nothing I can do to add to or detract from that love.

MARY GRAHAM,
The Greatest Lesson I've Ever Learned

*We catch a glimpse of
God in Grandma's love. . .*

"We are all very anxious to be understood, and it is very hard not to be. But there is one thing much more necessary."

"What is that, Grandmother?"

"To understand other people". . . . The lady pressed her once more to her bosom, saying:

"Do not be afraid, my child."

"No, Grandmother," answered the princess.

GEORGE MACDONALD,
The Princess and the Goblin

$\mathcal{I}$ am above eighty years old. . .I have been forty years a slave and forty years free, and would be here forty years more to have equal rights for all. I suppose I am kept here because something remains for me to do; I suppose I am yet to help to break the chain. . . . I want to keep things stirring, now that the ice is cracked.

SOJOURNER TRUTH, 1870

There are two ways of spreading light: to be the candles or the mirror that reflects it.

EDITH WHARTON

Grandmothers Make Us Remember

I have two grandmothers who are bright lights among the constellations of all the world's grandmothers. There is, of course, the basic grandmother stuff: decades of savory cooking from biscuits and gravy to fresh catfish and black-eyed peas, the diligent needle and thread work (I had the best embroidered cowboy shirts of any eleven-year-old, and nothing keeps the body warm like an heirloom afghan blanket), there are the ten-dollar checks on birthdays, which gradually get bigger but are always worth more than face value because they make one think; of all things Grandma. It is grandmas that make wonder.

A grandmother makes us remember what real pecan pie smells like, that restaurant peach cobbler didn't make us the men we are today, that old dogs in the yard still remember us and crave a good squirrel chase, that a "mega-mall" Christmas doesn't rate next to gift wrapping with the paper saved from years before, making all past Christmases present at once.

Grandmothers remind us of the importance of family, hard work, saving all we can, the centrality of home and, for many people, grandmothers are the preservers of the faith.

DANIEL DiGRIZ,
Conway, Arkansas

Behold,
I send you forth as sheep
in the midst of wolves:
be ye therefore wise as serpents,
and harmless as doves.

Matthew 10:16

Grandma's Church

In the corner of my grandmother's parlor stood an old pump organ. I sat on the round, wind-up stool and long before I had my first music lesson, I picked out "Abide With Me" by ear.

The special moment came when it was time to have "church." I chose a "text," prepared a "sermon," and decided upon the hymns. Then it was time to begin.

Grandma served as the "congregation," and her favorite wicker chair as the "pew." A makeshift lectern and altar completed the decor. Yours truly served as the organist, the preacher, and the usher who took the offering. (Every church service must have an offering.)

I remember her singing each stanza of the hymns I played, listening to me read from the Bible and preach my "sermon," and praying the Lord's Prayer, and, oh yes, putting her offering in the basket.

Those moments, melded together with a multitude of other meaningful memories, became the foundation that supported me through high school, college, seminary, and to this day.

THE REVEREND CARL HENKEL,
pastor at Mt. Olive Lutheran Church,
St. Paul, Minnesota

Gladys Taber was author of many books. Her "Blackberry Wisdom" column ran in the *Ladies Home Journal* for several years.

I often think of all the people who lived and loved, were happy or sad, those who were born and those who died in this [two-hundred-year-old] house. For there is a continuity of living if your house has sheltered its own down the long sweep of years. In our turn, we have cherished it, warmed it, and it offered us days rich with contentment. It has given us back-breaking hours of work and the satisfaction of tangible results from our work. It has given us fire on the hearth on long evenings, spring sunlight through the windows, cool moonlight on the doorsills in autumn.

This is a small house, but wide enough for fifteen cockers, two cats, an Irish setter, children growing up, friends who drop in overnight and stay three weeks.

The story of our life is written in the white tulips set in the Quiet Garden, in tomatoes ripening on the vine, in puppies bouncing through the great snowdrifts. It is inscribed with the scent of dark purple lilacs, the satiny touch of eggplant, the swift falling of golden leaves.

As seasons come to our gentle valley, Stillmeadow is always our personal adventure in happiness.

GLADYS TABER,
Stillmeadow

*Grandmother looked at me,
and through the wrinkles of her drawn smile
showed me how many ways she loved me.*

THOMAS CLARY

Two Grandmothers

My maternal grandmother was a schoolteacher from 1920 till after World War II. She'd retired from the classroom, but never grew weary of instructing. When I was about four years old she taught me to spell the word "pie" by forming the letters with fork tines in the top crust as she prepared it for the oven. It was a wonderful object lesson.

When in my late twenties I contracted a virus that left me partially paralyzed for a few weeks, my dad's mother especially warmed my heart. She only lived across town, but she took the time to mail me get-well cards several days in a row. The one that really made an impression on me was bright yellow and it unfolded and then unfolded some more. I remember laughing with delight by the time I had the whole thing opened up. What a treat!

ROBERTA CHRISTENSEN

Love and Spaghetti

"I knew you were coming," Grandmom would say, "because I heard a whistle. So I made macaroni."

We never figured out what (or Who?) made Grandmom hear these mysterious "whistles." But we believed her. The savory aroma greeting us at the door was proof enough.

My grandmother expressed her love through food. For example, each New Year's Day, Grandmom rose early to start a big pot of spaghetti "gravy", Italian sausage, meatballs, and the fixings for fried dough. Her windows on Broad Street gave us toasty front seats to Philadelphia's Mummers' Parade. Less fortunate people lined the curbs, shivering in bone-chilling weather.

Throughout the day, a constant flow of relatives and friends found warmth, happy conversations, and full bellies at Grandmom's bountiful table. If any strangers stood on her porch steps to watch the parade, Grandmom welcomed them in for coffee and a hot meal. Many sailors stationed at the Philadelphia Naval Base defrosted frozen hands and feet and filled growling stomachs in her kitchen. They experienced, along with the rest of us, the delicious comfort of a plate of spaghetti served with Grandmom's love.

EMILY KING, Oregon

*A woman is like a teabag,
you can not tell how strong she is
until you put her in hot water.*

NANCY REAGAN

The relationship between a grandmother and granddaughter is a special relationship. It's teaching, telling, giving, and bonding. It's learning family histories and traditions, things that have been passed from generation to generation. It's love shared.

FRANCINE HASKINS

Tribute to a Grandmother

As one of the Raiders' two fifth-round draft picks, linebacker Roderick Coleman says his grandmother, Alma Brown, became his legal guardian at a young age and since then the two have formed a special bond.

"She's a strong black woman who will do anything to survive, and I'm just like her," said Coleman, who moved in with her into what he described as "a bad neighborhood in Philadelphia." Yet as tough as his surroundings were, Coleman was an honor student in high school and set a record at East Carolina with thirty-nine career sacks. He credits his grandmother for giving him inspiration and encouragement on and off the football field.

"We're pretty close," he said. "I talk to her once or twice a week. She's my best friend and my role model."

JIM JENKINS, *Sacramento Bee*

The future belongs to those who believe in the beauty of their dreams.

ELEANOR ROOSEVELT: mother, grandmother, First Lady of the United States, 1932-1945, special ambassador to the United Nations and "Good Will Ambassador" from the U.S. to many nations.

My Grandmother's Love Letters

*T*here are no stars tonight
But those of memory.
Yet how much room for memory there is
In the loose girdle of soft rain.
There is even room enough
For the letters of my mother's mother,
Elizabeth,
That have been pressed so long

Into a corner of the roof
That they are brown and soft
And liable to melt as snow.

Over the greatness of such space
Steps must be gentle.
It is all hung by an invisible
  white hair.
It trembles as birch limbs webbing
  the air.
And I ask myself,
"Are your fingers long enough to play
Old keys that are but echoes:
Is the silence strong enough

A Grandmother spreads sunshine wherever she goes...

To carry back the music to its source
And back to you again
As though to her?"
Yet I would lead my grandmother by the hand
Through much of what she would not understand;
And so I stumble. And the rain continues on the roof
With such a sound of gently pitying laughter.

HART CRANE, 1892–1932

Love does not just sit there,
like a stone;
it has to be made, like bread,
remade all the time, made new.

URSULA LE GUIN

Grandmother's Passover Popovers

½ cup shortening

1 ½ cups water

1 ½ cups matzo meal

½ tsp. salt

1 tbsp. sugar

7 eggs

Heat shortening and water until shortening is dissolved. Add matzo meal, salt, and sugar and stir until mixture no longer sticks to the side of pan. Remove from heat and cool well. Beat eggs into mixture, one at a time. Spoon into a well-greased muffin pan, popover pan, or Pyrex custard cup until almost full. Bake in preheated oven at 400° for about 50 minutes. Makes 12 or 13.

KENNETH KULLER

Grandma Great

Grandma Great was born a slave in rural Kentucky, seven years before the end of the American Civil War. Shortly after her birth she was sold, along with the rest of her family, to a farmer in southern Illinois, where she grew up, fell in love, married, bore ten children, became a grandmother, then, of course, a great-grandmother. Family legend has it that, when she was five years old, Abraham Lincoln saw her in a crowd and was so charmed by her smile he stopped what he was doing, walked over and picked her up and bounced her in his arms. If the story is true—and I'm sure that it is—it is interesting that the man who is credited with ending slavery in America probably had no idea that the blond, blue-eyed little girl he held in his arms was born a mulatto Negro slave only a few years earlier.

REED YARROW

Grandma's Kitchen

In grandma's kitchen
the light over the sink
spilled life into
steamy darkness
through the night,
a safeguarding beacon
for sleeping and wakeful,
drawn as a magnet
to sweet rewards,
the haloed luminance
in secret
revealed.

P. L. MAKOLONDRA

The Grandmothers' Grandmother

It comes to us all, every woman,
its guises many:
lingering illness,
children grown,
perhaps a job that no longer matters.

We weren't expecting it:
the knock at the door,
a stranger,
yet,
in some uncanny way,
familiar:
like a memory from lifetimes ago.

An ancient crone beckons us;
we go,
feeling uncertain.
Her arms reach out in welcome.
We melt into her comforting warmth.
The destination of this journey
is the same for each:

time to let go,
mother no more.

How different we feel,
distanced,
as if watching the lives around us
from afar.
In our heart the love is there,
just as always,
yet changed somehow.

Though compassion remains;
no longer do we try,
futilely,
to fix:
people's lives;
relationships;
people's hearts.

We offer love,
encouragement,
our prayers:
the rest we leave to them.

ANNE JOHNSON

When this book began, my grandson Adam asked Andrew what a runcible spoon was, and Andrew said he'd ask me, because I was very wise. A runcible spoon is one with slots or piercings, so that liquid will not stay in it. Such a spoon is used for cranberry sauce, fish. . .or mince and slices of quince.

KRISTEN JOHNSON INGRAM

The price of wisdom is above rubies.

Job 28:1